EXCITING OUTDOOR CAREERS

ZOOLOGIST

DWAYNE HICKS

PowerKiDS press.

Published in 2026 by The Rosen Publishing Group, Inc.
2544 Clinton Street, Buffalo, NY 14224

First Edition

Editor: Greg Roza
Book Design: Rachel Rising

Photo Credits: Cover, Liukov/Shutterstock.com; Cover, pp. 1, 3–24 klyaksun/Shutterstock.com; Cover, pp. 1, 3–24 Iurii Vlasenko/Shutterstock.com; p. 4 FamVeld/Shutterstock.com; p. 5 schusterbauer.com/Shutterstock.com; p. 7 huang jenhung/Shutterstock.com; p. 9 brunocoelho/Shutterstock.com; p. 10 ScottYellox/Shutterstock.com; p. 11 VagrantDragon/Shutterstock.com; p. 13 pingpongcha_photo/Shutterstock.com; p. 14 Sergii Figurnyi/Shutterstock.com; p. 15 KARI K/Shutterstock.com; p. 17 YegoroV/Shutterstock.com; p. 18 spatuletail/Shutterstock.com; p. 19 dom zara/Shutterstock.com; p. 20 encierro/Shutterstock.com; p. 21 Danny Ye/Shutterstock.com.

Cataloging-in-Publication Data

Names: Hicks, Dwayne.
Title: Zoologist / Dwayne Hicks.
Description: Buffalo, New York : PowerKids Press, 2026. | Series: Exciting outdoor careers | Includes glossary and index.
Identifiers: ISBN 9781499457308 (pbk.) | ISBN 9781499457315 (library bound) | ISBN 9781499457322 (ebook)
Subjects: LCSH: Zoologists–Juvenile literature. | Zoologists–Vocational guidance–Juvenile literature.
Classification: LCC QL50.5 H54 2026 | DDC 590.92–dc23

Manufactured in China

CPSIA Compliance Information: Batch #QWPK26. For Further Information contact Rosen Publishing at 1-800-237-9932.

CONTENTS

WIDE WORLD OF ANIMALS

Do you love all kinds of animals? Not just some, but all of them? Some people like cats or dogs. Some people like fish, and others like birds. But there are those who simply love all animals! You might be surprised to hear that there's a career for people who love animals. Zoology is the scientific study and understanding of animals. This includes their biology, behaviors, **habitats**, and much more.

Many zoologists are outdoors workers. That's where most wild animals are! Zoologists may work in and around forests, deserts, rainforests, oceans, and other habitats. Read on to learn more about this exciting career choice.

Zoologists work in many different types of places, depending on the animal they are studying. They also work in labs, government offices, fisheries, and zoos, to name a few.

BRANCHES OF ZOOLOGY

While it's true that zoologists often have an interest in different kinds of animals, many choose to specialize in a specific branch of zoology. This could be based on a single type of animal or animal group, such as reptiles, insects, primates, or rodents.

Marine biologists are zoologists who are experts in ocean life. Animal behaviorists study animal behavior and interactions. Wildlife ecologists study the interactions between animals and their habitats. Ornithologists study birds. Entomologists study insects. Ichthyologists study fish. These are just a few specialties. There are far too many to mention here. If you can think of an animal, there's a branch for it!

OUTDOOR ADVICE

Scientists who study plants are known as botanists. Scientists who study the interactions between plants, animals, and their habitats are called ecologists, environmentalists, or conservationists.

Large, thick-skinned mammals that have hoof-like feet (such as elephants) are called pachyderms. So, a zoologist who studies pachyderms is a pachydermatologist!

EDUCATION AND TRAINING

Most zoologist jobs require at least a four-year college degree. To earn a zoology degree, students are expected to understand animal biology, which includes animal cells, **anatomy**, body processes, life cycles, and more. Classes will also include physics and math. In addition to classwork, zoology students also research topics, work in labs, and work in the field. Many colleges offer zoology **internships**, which can help students get a start in the field.

In time, most zoology students choose a specialty. This is usually something they're **passionate** about, such as a specific animal species (or kind), animal behaviors, animal classification, and much more.

OUTDOOR ADVICE

Zoologists can join one or more professional organizations, such as The Wildlife Society and the Zoological Association of America. Associations help zoologists in many ways.

These zoology students are learning about ring-tailed lemurs at a zoo in Poland.

ANIMAL WELFARE AND MANAGEMENT

A zoologist's greatest skill is studying animals and their behaviors. They observe animals in the wild and sometimes in **captivity**. They record what they observe, which includes what animals eat, how and when they sleep, interactions within the group and with other animal groups, and their ways of staying safe. Zoologists sometimes collect **specimens** to be studied later in a lab.

The information zoologists collect is used to help improve the wellbeing of animals. A zoologist working in a state park may notice the number of beavers has decreased steadily over the past five years. Identifying and helping to fix problems like this is called wildlife management.

Beavers are considered keystone species in most environments. This means they play an important role in the overall health of all animals in a habitat. If they were to disappear, many other species would suffer.

HABITAT PROTECTORS

In addition to studying animals, zoologists also study their habitats. This helps them learn even more about the animals that live there. When a habitat is healthy, that means the plants and animals within it are healthy too. Healthy habitats are considered balanced, meaning that they support many species and no populations grow too large or small.

Zoologists monitor healthy habitats to make sure they aren't being damaged. Depending on the location, they may work with other scientists, civil engineers, urban planners, and local officials to help protect animals' homes. Some zoologists are trained to help restore damaged habitats to balanced, healthy locations.

OUTDOOR ADVICE

Zoologists and habitat specialists are often involved when towns and cities create new public spaces, such as skate parks and splash pads. They make sure new projects don't hurt local animals or habitats.

These zoologists are testing a local water source for pollution.

TEACHING AND ENTERTAINING

Sometimes scientists want to share their knowledge with others. There are several ways a zoologist can do this. The first is by becoming a high school or college teacher. Teachers inspire the next generation of scientists! Zoologists are also hired to educate the public about local wildlife and habitats through public outreach programs.

Zoos, aquariums, and animal **sanctuaries** hire zoologists to monitor and even care for animals of all kinds. Some are hired to lead educational programs, and others are hired to lead entertaining shows. This is a great chance to show off zoological knowledge while entertaining crowds of sightseers.

This zoo worker is an ornithologist—a bird expert. He is teaching a crowd of zoo visitors all about the bald eagle.

CONSERVATION LEADERS

Conservation is the planned management of natural resources, wildlife, and wilderness areas to keep them from being misused or damaged. Everyone has some responsibility to think about conservation issues. Zoologists, however, often take the lead when it comes to conservation. This is called stewardship.

Zoologists are wildlife problem solvers. They protect **endangered** species. They identify, monitor, and remove **invasive species**. They help fisheries to maintain healthy fish populations. They help communities develop plans and procedures for new construction projects as well as wilderness cleanup projects. They keep pollution created by human activities from harming wildlife and habitats.

OUTDOOR ADVICE

One conservation issue that zoologists deal with is poaching. This is the illegal hunting of protected animal species. It's a serious problem throughout the world.

U.S. national parks are protected wilderness areas. They are home to thousands of species of animals. Zoologists help other workers, especially park rangers, keep park wildlife safe and healthy.

FAMOUS ZOOLOGISTS

In 1967, American Dian Fossey created a research center in Rwanda, Africa, to study the mountain gorilla. Fossey observed mountain gorillas and even became good friends with them! Fossey's efforts greatly increased our understanding of mountain gorillas' behavior, **communication**, and social structure. Fossey also led a battle against mountain gorilla poachers.

DIAN FOSSEY WITH MOUNTAIN GORILLAS

You've probably heard of some of Attenborough's greatest documentaries, including *Life on Earth, The Living Planet, The Blue Planet*, and *Planet Earth*.

David Attenborough is a British **naturalist** and conservationist. He has been making and staring in nature movies since 1954! For seven decades, Attenborough has used storytelling mixed with amazing film of animals in their natural habitats to teach people all over the world about zoology, wild animals, and conservation.

THE RIGHT JOB FOR ME?

Becoming a zoologist takes hard work and lots of schooling. However, the hard work pays off! The average pay for zoology jobs is about $70,000, but you can expect to make $100,000 or more as you gain more experience. About 67 percent of all zoologists in the United States work for the government, and those jobs often pay better.

Zoologists have many jobs to choose from! They work in schools, zoos, parks, and cities. They explore forests, rivers, beaches, and many other habitats. They work with teachers, scientists, city planners, and—of course—animals! What's the perfect zoologist job for you?

This zoologist is feeding a group of spider monkeys in a zoo in Singapore.

GLOSSARY

anatomy: A branch of science that deals with the structure of animals.

captivity: The state of living somewhere controlled by humans—such as in a zoo or an aquarium—instead of in the wild.

communication: The use of words, sounds, signs, or behaviors to convey ideas, thoughts, and feelings.

endangered: In danger of dying out.

habitat: The natural home for plants, animals, and other living things.

internship: A job done—often without pay—in order to gain experience.

invasive species: Plants or animals from one area that spread quickly in a new area and harm native plants and animals.

naturalist: A specialist in natural history.

passionate: Showing or expressing strong feeling.

sanctuary: A safe place for wildlife to live where hunting is illegal.

specimen: Something taken from the natural world for study in a lab.

FOR MORE INFORMATION

BOOKS

DK Staff. *Eyewitness Encyclopedia of Animals*. New York, NY: DK Eyewitness, 2025.

Mason, Paul. *Animal Kingdom*. Buffalo, NY: Enslow Publishing, 2025.

WEBSITES

Dian Fossey
www.biography.com/scientists/dian-fossey
Read more about the life of Dian Fossey and her courageous and groundbreaking work with mountain gorillas.

David Attenborough
www.biography.com/movies-tv/david-attenborough
This website offers more information about Attenborough and his long list of accomplishments.

INDEX